T0127422

nick demske

nick demske

selected for the
Fence Modern Poets Series
by Joyelle McSweeney

albany, new york

©Nick Demske 2010, 2011
All rights reserved.

Cover design by Rebecca Wolff
Book layout by Colie Collen

Published in the United States by

Fence Books
Science Library 320
University at Albany
1400 Washington Avenue
Albany, NY 12222
www.fenceportal.org

Fence Books are printed in Canada by Westcan Printing Group   www.westcanpg.com
and distributed by University Press of New England   www.upne.com

Library of Congress Cataloguing in Publication Data
        Demske, Nick [1983-]
        Nick Demske/Nick Demske

Library of Congress Control Number: 2010937695

ISBN 13: 978-1-934200-39-1

FIRST EDITION
10 9 8 7 6 5 4 3

FENCE BOOKS are published in partnership with the University at Albany and the New
York State Writers Institute, and with help from the New York State Council on the Arts
and the National Endowment for the Arts.

CONTENTS

ACKNOWLEDGMENTS

Major thanks go to the following publications—as well as their editors— in which some of these poems originally appeared: *Action Yes, Artful Dodge, Arsenic Lobster, Conduit, DMQ Review, Expose Kenosha, Express Milwaukee, Fact-Simile, Humble Humdrum Cotton Frock, Knock, Make, Monkey Puzzle, Moria, Sawbuck, Seven Corners, Spirits* and *Thieves Jargon*. The poem "Hot Dog" also appeared in a review on Philip Metres' blog, *Behind the Lines*.

NICK DEMSKE writes from culture like the Hollywood version of a rebellious slave, the role shredding off him, culture's synthetic exemplary tales shredding and piling up on the floor of the projector room, but non-biodegradable, sticking around, the pancake makeup also strangely persisting, rendering his face plastic and one with the material of the film, the celluloid itself. How can we tell this dancer from his nasty dance? Language has ecstatic prison sex in these narrow cells, de-synchs and hooks up in detrimental sequences which will make the baby sick; the sonnet form both persists and shreds, goes on talking/being a talkie; his own name copies itself again and again like a one-man "I am Spartacus"—splits like a wascally wabbit before the Law. One lump or two? Or, the sonnet is one brief sequence played backwards and forwards until its fake, twitchy face says everything: "This poem is named after you, like a slave." "Nick Demske, you are everything wrong with the world. Which is to say: the wor/Ld." Is it shit or is it speech? Is Language the patented dance move of the sapiens sapiens or the catchy scat that shows where we've passed? The staff or the shit of life? "This humor so dark you mistake/It for chocolate." "God wins because he's bigger,/Until I digest this cracker, converting it on/Into the drabbest defecant His face will ever don." Yum yum! A poet both coprophilic and narcissistic finds his own face reflected in some pretty dirty places. Or, as Catherine Clément has held, "To eat the placenta, one's excrement, or one's Dasein, to devour the loved one with kisses or to make love with God: these are some of the possible equivalences to the body's debris. The angel is part of it, as is the beast that follows him like a shadow since Pascal united them, one behind the other in an ineluctable procession." Or, per Demske, "I enjambed that promise/So far up the Muse's tuchis he still shits shards of meter." "Ick, narcotica prissy self-gratified non-prophet: AWE SHIT." —Joyelle McSweeney

I.

IN VOCATION

HARLEM TECTONICA

for Michael Bernstein

> *"me, wag."*
> —John Berryman

Rumba, paintmixer. Make the rafters sing, the picture frames chatter their walls.
The infants confused for electric maracas. Stripped naked and locked
In the winter.   The carefully crenulated gears fall from their hinges, paintmixer. Til all s
Crews shimmy loose of their thread slots.

The platform quakes for the train like a lover
Or someone really really afraid. Scream at the altar
In tongues, paintmixer, the jumper cables of the spirit
Jolting your torso like an unfit parent

In the night—Why won't you stop crying, paintmixer, cry
Ing tambourine tremors through the fault
Lines, through submachine hands barely legal enough to fuck I finger fuck this light
Socket like a paintmixer bimbo asthenic with chortledom   Why

Are you in me, paintmixer? Why your alligator teeth sinking so into these nipples,
These nerves,   flood ignition   Be *still*.

2.

LET THE CARTOONS BEGIN

COMMON SENSE

"the very word is like a bell"
                            —*John Keats*

I didn't think it was loaded. But it was a kn
Ife. So we're *both* right. I foresee
Blinding enlightenment. I beat these children like the deadest of horsies.
The people cheer at their victory. Peasants dan

Cing in gutters, commoners singing like so many
Semi-trucks braking. This is the ultra-vulgarity to they who make
The definitions. This is cops getting shot in abnormally
Broad daylight. I will make me beautiful if it takes

Uglying everything else; a reflect
Ion so unfamiliar you feel impolite confronting it. I am the awestruck lex
Icographers, staring back into a nightingale. I will beat these
Precious children back to life. Fuck me, shit me.

Remind me what it's like to be offended, Nick Demske.
Ah.   Already with thee.

MY NAME IS

"The sight of the flames maddens me with pleasure"
— *Walt Whitman*

Unsanitized hypodermia. Full dorsal poetry. Homos say
What. Say *what?* Say *when*.   I'm going to buttfuck
You in the mouth. I know where you live. I pause between tracks,
Betraying my inauthenticity. Como se

Llamas? Teething ring. Angel machine. Caution:
Moving walkway ends now. Warning: may contain
Nuts. Drive-thru   liquor store. Same sex
Divorce rate. Where do I sign? Why don't I slip   into something a little more

More more more.   The sticker on his breast pocket
Reads "Superlative Obscenity," translated un
Iversally. Conglomerate vulgarity.   C'mon, party people. I dare you to jump.
My touch turns gold into animate objects.

This is nomenclature reclamation declaration take one.   Redefinition. But
The lexicographers respond, defiant and unison.   What?

WHETHER MY HEAD OR THIS WALL
WILL BE FIRST TO SURRENDER
after Paul Ruebens

They don't have a name for what I am.
Age appropriate   sex symbol.   Cup full of athlete,
Spilling.   Huffing mouth-to-mouth at a carrion
Heap, petting these bunnies to pieces.   Day breaks like a he

Art in your hands, Nick Demske.   You stammer
Dactylic excuses.   The dendrophile tweezes his splinters post-
Coitus. My CPR
Plows through a sternum.   When I say "post-

Apocalyptic,"   I mean "contemporary."
In a big, big way.   And you've been working
In a media that does not yet exist.   These spasms, unfounded—visiting
Hours are over and the majority

Of your traits does not adhere to my culture's standards
Of beauty: Recklessness. Renaissance. Nicholas.   You give new meaning to the word

TREASURE

We now return you to your regularly scheduled pogrom.
When I get all steamed up I will shoot.
Show me angry   regular plus or premium.
Propagandist cavatine make me poot.

(Poot).   The complaint department is really a make
Believe mousetrap. The screwdriver is really a butter knife.
The complaint department is the pin of a fake
Grenade. Just wait until you see my other wife.

(Poot).   A man and a woman are lesbians together.
The scrivener lives without
Dining. Aretha Franklin's voice is a National Treasure.
I don't know what I think about

That. I don't know what I think
About. I don't know what I think.

WORDS WILL NEVER

for Nicholas Michael Ravnikar

> *"but only heaven hangs over him foul"*
> —*Berryman*

We demand accessible poetry, but our access prances home
Denied. We squirrels bury nuts never to be exhumed.
I hope you're happy. Now think about what you've done.
I love what you've done

With the place, with the splintery, flammable porch.
We demand handicap accessible poetry, but the ramps slant too steep, the doors
All too narrow. My precious precious
Mongo—I observe you from a distance like a holiday no one else celebrates.   You catalyst

Of illiteracy rates, you hissy fit for a king.
Not only are you deaf, but you sound retarded
When you talk. O brother. Either I've sharted
Abstractions more substance than art or a baby with nothing

To say is learning to speak. No
One has any idea what the fuck you're talking about. Let go.

CENTERED

Expression medicates conscious awareness. Sufficient
Knowledge of esteem *inflicted* same.   Pity ish. Righteous preservation
Taught destructive importance; made man-improvement.
Employed fulfilling prophecy, cleaning oven. Image/less/realization.

O moi am soliloquoy masturbation narcissist.
Solitaire. Samizdat. Single play
Er…piano? Confinement, Roy-
Al (one), we solipsist.

Erotic biographies belay fellatio. Mate
Lyze. Motive: some psy didact-matic.
Bus, bahn, chthon…graph inoculation! Intoxicate
Pilot-mobile, kinetic.

Believe in your denial, mythologist. Serve harp
Hypnosis to thine own indulgence.   Help.

SECTION C.

PUT YOUR FACE IN MY TONGUE

Nobody move. Read them and weep. Lifeguard on duty
Like you've never seen him before. Verily,
Yea, I saith unto thee: a meadow of summer
Fruit, a damsel with a dulcimer

The many dappled scimitar of sky thy lips art cleft
At. Nobody is moved like a crime scene invest
Igation. Like poetry too complex to be beautiful. Reader,
Ideal if a little unliterate, is your refrigerator running from the refrigerator

Police? Are your standards daintily lowered upon this catafalque
Love?   If I ever dislodge this rock,
I'm having a party and you're not invited.   *Read them*, fine
As the font which binds them, and weep, bitterly, at the grammar they defile.

It's Nick Demske like you've never seen him
Before; loins clothed—an angel crowning an ivory mausoleum.

TRAGIC SONGSTRESS
for Angela

"Have things gone terribly wrong?" the sumo
Inquires of his 14th helping. In Japanese though.
"Am I a total douchebag?" pontificates the scholar,
Addressing his robe. In Latin though.   I reinvent the solar

Powered flash light   every night. I malfunct
Ion like an elapsed **R&B** singer's wardrobe.
"Have I neither rhythm nor blues?" reflects
A bare breasted negress in spotlight.   The dendraphobe

Muses, "This poem has no theme, direction
Or valid interpretation," and, then, vomits an **R&B** lyric.   "Have I wasted my prover
Bial life?" he asks a random turd in a mountain of scat.   In every scholar
There's a natural secretion

Waiting to smell sort of gross. In every **R&B** poet, readvent of dirge.
In every sumo, there's a little bulimic awaiting a glorious purge.

HOTDOG

Does this fanny pack make me look fat?
No, but it makes you look like a big fucking idiot.
And, also, slightly fat, yes.   I have no idea what a hot
Dog is made of. If you're going to act like a brat,

I'm going to eat you like one. Why feign this as coincidence? Why don
Ate your body to science when it could feed
An entire village? I want to lick you in places that would leave
My tongue bacterial.   Does this hard won

Prosperity make me look fat? This humor so dark you mistake
It for chocolate.
Nick Demske, you are everything wrong with the world. Which is to say: the wor
Ld. Share with me your most secret ingredients.   This megamart once was a for

Est. These teeth marks, once a kiss. Do these priorit
Ies make me look fat, these scars, these explosives beneath my sweatshirt?

BREAKDOWN

for JB

Spontaneous combustions, once predicted, quee
F into the mouth of demotion. Predicting combustions of the spontaneous
Phylum revokes their very license like a very license
Re-vo-ker. You've failed me. Me

Aning I will repeat your course next semester, these scantron
Bubbles idiotically reflecting my demoticon
Gawk. You're ruining the ending like a pre
Mature apocalypse. You suck at life. Your combustion lacks spontaneity,

Nick Demske. Thus, you are the lobster
Bib of poetry, reaching anti-climax in the generation
Of every unplanned pregnancy. Irregular weather patterns. Meteor
O-logistics. I could've told you this was going to happen. Combustion's

So predictable.   *Can I take them to the bridge?*
Take them to the bridge.

THE BRIDGE

"Keep smiling the boss away"
                    —Hart Crane

Now this product here should have been recalled p
Ages ago. Nothing a little duct
Tape won't fix, right? But lo! Besight thy barometer lect
Ures, these intimate sui-soliloquies.

No animals were harmed during this poem's composition.
However, outrageous scores of humanoid abortions at its unveiling.
This shouldn't have happened, this. Self-fulfilling
Prophecy in the sense of chronic masturbation.

We give away the punch line in our first
Mortal utteri. What did you expect
Orate?   And now, forecasted or not, the bats
Storm the belfry, the thunderheads clap, the dingle-flavored berries, uncle-climact

Ick, narcotica prissy self-gratified non-prophet:
AWE SHIT.

EVERYTHING PERSONAL

Make all checks payable to: the artist formerly known as.
Take all proper precautions, as in Ken Doll's gonads.
Try it, you'll like it. I'm a grown ass
Man bitch. Mind your own. I'm a lady in the streets and so nas

Ty in bed you'll swear you fucked the whole goddamned freak
Factory.   We're sorry, the last lines of poetry you read were chief
Ly mistranslated by Indonesian laborers. They employ for cheap-
Er than domestic manufacturers. They speak

Pillow talk as a second language. We're sorry, the deductible
Doesn't match the co-pay. We're sorry, your son's unstable.
We're sorry, that number has been disconnected.   We're delectable
And nutritious! We're Dr. Love. We're Dr. Kevorkian. We're Dr. Huckstable.

We're Dr. Frankenstein. We're really sorry. Please don't try to face this.
Does anyone here mind if I tell a joke that's a little racist?

SCARE TACTIC

"You defend a city lost in flames."
                    —Virgil

You are now witnessing the most tragic
Origins to: The Poetry of Intimidation! (Boo). Anthrax
In the mailbox, explosives in the sneakers. Jihad in the thorax
And a *Philosophiae Doctor* in Kamikaze Aerobatics.

And Marketing. Give me that lunch money, say uncle
Samson, prices may vary, offer redeemable while supplies
Are limited. Who broadcasted the clip national
For three months on a loop? Who feltched barrel sized

Hits of premium from the country club's poo-nanny?
You. I. We syphon a leper's last artery
United, yes; the poet! There's a new terrorist
Catwalking the plank, matey. I just want to talk. I just

Want the children. I just want a few barnstormer
Shits and giggles, primarily the former.

WILL NOT BE TELEVISED

Virginia Tech, April '07

The world is flat. The Nick Demske
Is hot. Please drink Nick Demske responsibly.
What happens when a spin-off spins
Back on? Do we observe a moment of silence?

Do we take a moment to silence all cell
Phones and electronic devices? I'm severely depressed whenever I pay attention.
I'm really fucking angry about everything. I straddle
Nick Demske between my thighs til he spills and scorches my million

Dollar lap. This wheelchair is going nowhere, slowly,
Like a joke so practical you forget to laugh. Figuratively.
The world is flat and can't afford
Implants. Do you copy, Nick Demske? You figure of speech, you're

Sorry you ever asked.
Are you paying attention? Is it spinning back on?   Smile. You've just been
        Nick Demsked.

RHETORICAL PRAYER

"Is man no more than this?"

I took off my makeup; a slug drenched in Lot's
Wife's ashes. An overactive sympathy gland. Keep out
Of reach of children. Limit one per survivor. Carve
Your lover's name into my bark.

Woof. I took off my clothes and under
Neath—a rainbow so diverse in its beauty it rivals the homeland secur
Ity color scheme. The answer to all those rhet
Orical questions. All those rhetorical quests.

I took off my skin: a garbage
Can full of recyclables. Hard boiled   fabergé.
I took off my bones. There are no rhetorical questions. Only rhetorical
Prayers, digging beneath their sepulchral

Words to excavate your own.   I ripped out my stuffing.
Removed guts, veins, organs. And then: Nothing.

AS FAR AWAY

"mortals were careful [then] and never forsook the shores of their homelands."
                                                                    —*Ovid*

The Holocaust never existed. What are you going to do
About it? The Holocaust never happened, but your mother's autopsy reveals
It can if you just believe. To
Page this person, press five now. All sales fatal. All sales

Symbolically representative of mortality. I know a woman so redolent
Of pulchritude you'd contract second
Hand erectile dysfunction from the mere hint of her figment.
The Holocaust never happened. Better luck next time. A woman

So pulchritudinous you want to turn away, as far away
As humanly possible. I meant to do that. For old time's sake. When
You're finished recording, please hang up and try
Again. God is of not much use here, like a lesbian

So beautiful she turns gay men
Straight. I don't believe in the Holocaust.   Amen.

SOMETHING IN MY THIRD

I am the I   in team. I am the hallucination in the Ror
Shack. I am the sugar
In the gas tank of the itty bitty short
Bus. What do you see when you close your

Eyes? Does the sun cast its honeyed
Rays through slaughterhouse windows? Are two cell
Mates submitting to the ecstasy
Of love? I am the girl in the boy's bathroom. I am an unheal

Thy dependence on anaphora.
When I wake from this coma
What first will I say?   There is a girl in
The boy's bathroom. There is a field glossed in

Sunlight and the breeze breathes like a lover. There's something
I need to say.   There is no I in team.

FAUX HAWK

for Dave Haynes

No is the new yes; hence the chic chip on this trapezius.
It matches my eyes, my first person limita
Tions. It complements my insults. Its sassy little number's neutral, potentially hazardous
By extension. The cashier tells us to have a good day.

But it's night. And we take this personally.
Night is the new day. I am violently Nick Demske, the pissy,
Second-hand trench coat of poetry. Behold my clearance discounts. I we
Ar my Nick Demske like a burkha—the lamb's wool codpiece, pessi

Mystic. I once wrote a death letter to a childhood pen pal. Now I write
Death letters to everyone, indiscriminate. You, sir, write
Love letters to no one.   How common.
No is the new yes, justifying our mutual molestations. Our denomin

Ator lies in faux pas, dysfashion, dysfunction. But this is a pact, in
Which I swear to write defective odes to someone I still don't hate, feigning satisfaction.

AS A DOG RETURNETH TO HIS VOMIT

On my mother's grave. On all things holy.
On my firstborn child's virginity.   On the rebound, Nick Demske—
You smell like Lazarus returning in the form of
A cyclical argument. You smell like protesters burning Mein Kampf.

I promised myself I wouldn't cry. I stuck a needle
In my eye and all I got was this lousy needle.
In my eye. Please continue to hold and your prayer will
Be answered in the order 'twas received. Well

Look who's crawling back to the question   for forgiveness,
Take a look at relentless repentance. Just one won't hurt.   I promised
Myself I'd stop writing poems. I broke that promise.
I line broke that promise. I enjambed that promise

So far up the Muse's tuchis we still shit shards of meter. I drink from this vomit,
I'll barf in this vomit. I poured every last drop down the sink. I promise.

PSYCHE 101

"In some untrodden region of my mind"
                                   —Keats

The key to brainwashing is repetition. The key
Did you expect me to repeat that now? Did you expect me to
Enact the experience you think I describe?
But alas, I describe only an aggressive brand of hula. Behold my swivel

Ing hips. The key to brainwashing is kept beside
The porch in a hollow, plastic object designed to look like a rock. But brainwas
Hing was unlocked, unloaded. Unloved.   The pen *is,*
Indeed, mightier than the sword. But this is a gun against your head, an extension of my

Condolences. You will do and say exactly as we tell
You until we simply needn't tell you anymore. The key to brainwashing is next to
Godliness, getting further behind
The ears than you'd ever thought possible. Nick Demkse. Nick Demske. Plutoni

Ck Columbus McCarthy. III.   You're the spawn of expectation. You are the key t
O brainwashing. An historic reenactment. Lather, Rinse.   Lather.   Rinse.

SONNET

for Annette Duncan

Because I say it's poetry. So nanny
Nanna boo boo. What are these statistics
Based on?   A true stor
Y.   Imitation ice cream better than any ice
Cream you've ever tasted. Better at what you ask? Math, it replies.

And your bowels evacuate at the horror
Of a talking dessert.   I mean breakfast.   Because I say it's
Poetry. Because I am the substitute teacher, better than any
[insert six more lines here]

XI.

NOTICE

Inc ompliance with federal law, you are hereby
Notified that a pest control service application
May have been performed on this poem or certain, nearby
Poems of separate origin. Anything you say or do can

And will be used against you in an act of contrition;
Para Español, marque dos. I got an autographed edition
Of The Iliad off eBay. I got a father that weeps
At what's traditionally wept at. I want to eat

Your excretia. Women and children first, ma'am.
Paper or plastic? Dying or dead? Make up your mind, man.
This is an elegy, not an ode
And I, the highest priestess of this town commode,

Hereby defibrillate these cadavers for fun. I go
Pee in the sink. I dance. I sing. I love to say I told you so.

POP SONNET

for Ange

And what do you think about this piece? *I try not to think about art.* What's interesting
You most about this piece? *The shadow I'm casting*
Upon it. Damn: it feels good to be a gangster. It's snowing manna.
It   is raining men. Ha

Llelujah. A young person is smearing their privates
With a condiment and will shortly invite their pets
To remove it. My grandpa's name is grandpa. My life is ruined,
As are these shoes. What did you like most about the poem?

It was short.   You're my favorite work of art, cause every
Nobody gets you. Today   was a good day.
My muse gushes deafening orchestra that shreds into fleshy
Confetti. This poem is boring, and she's not okay

With that.   In the midnight hour. I can fee
L your power.   Down on my kneeeeees.

FIAT/ COUNTER-FIAT

for Angela

I'm faking it. For real. I actually have
No idea what the weather will be
Like. No evidence supports this augurment hab
It, this lip-synching lifeboat, these rhymes—forcibly

Espoused, nonconsenting. Fasten your seat belts
For an edge of your seat thriller. The most influential weaponry
Since sliced bread. Smile for me, daddy. You get what you pay for and surgeries
This plastique come at twelve

For ten coppers (read: "zincs").   I'm faking it. For serious. Unqualified,
Transgendered, forcing laughter at obtuse drollery as funny as the counter
Feit bills lining our G-strings. But it's *my* Tupperware party. I can cry
Wolf and blame the Tourette's until the motions gone through inspire

Orgasms so genuine we all forget our manners. The time,
Among other abstractions, has come. Now you've really crossed the line.

BORN AGAIN

"Tweet tweet," says the trans-species butterfly.
"Moo," says the dog who identifies as cow. I'm not a poet, I
Just write poetry. I'm not a cop killer, I just
Kill cops. I'm not a cop killer, I just

Write poetry. I'm allowed to use the word nigger,
Or variants thereof, because I'm in an inter
Racial relationship. It's my gift; my curse.   "Crack," says
The firecracker, perpetuating negative stereotypes.   The print vanishes,

Fine as hairs; a font so small only dogs can read it.   "Moo,"
They recite and advance to the slaughter.
I'm allowed to use the word "Nick Demkse" to
Mean "The Mighty Lake Erie" or "Holy Hobo's trash-fire night light."
   (cue laughter?)

I am not in God's will, meaning he revoked my inheritance.
And/or meaning I override omnipotence. "Ha," laughs the embarrassment.

ELEVEN

"Put your hands where I can see them," said the blind man.
And he picked up his ham
Mer and pulverized all my fingers. When no one attends this party, what will be done
With these eight meat lovers' pizzas? The question,

Rhetorical as Miranda rights. Put your
Hands where I can taste them you leprous freak, you pulverulent delicat
Essen. *I see men as trees, walking.* An arbor
Ist ushering. But with every laureate

Blacked out from pain, who retrieves the scattered dactyls?
The blind man questions authority, rhetor
Ically. Is heaven as lonely as it looks, officer?
How the fuck should I know. A show of hands please. The gavels

Descend. Ye lovers of meat, behold thy resurrection, thy
Resuscitation. How many fingers am I holding up? Rhetorically.

AND THE SYMBOL OF HIS COVENANT
SHALL DECORATE OUR SHIELDS

There is no peace, saith the Lord, unto the wicked.
Sorry to rain on your pride parade. The matri
Arch has come to terms   most derogatory, developmentally stunted.
The matriarch caught with his pants down, salty

As Lot's wife herself. God is a virgin,
Which explains a lot. God is a Christian,
Initiating full-blown **AIDS** like foreplay.
If the forbidden fruit tastes abominable, you're saved,

You're deviant, you're unnatural. I'm out. Peace be with you. Be not afraid.
It's just a stage. God is love, uncer
Tain restrictions may apply, void
Where prohibited, *This* is my alter

Ego, *This* is my altar boy, *This* is my two shekels.
The matriarch knows God. Personally.   In the biblical sense.

DID HE SMILE

That cloud looks just like the archetypal
Loss of innocence. I know where you keep the little key to your journal.
When the student reveals his bi
Sexuality, what bathroom ought we restrict it to? What the Fi

Re eater. Sword swallower. Pen regurgitator. How great a god mus
T be to have made such mistakes of infinitude.
Mother picks up in the midst of the prank call. The kind of sm
Ile that belongs on a milk carton. Tonight, I will convince you

To do something you once swore you'd never
Do. That cloud looks just like the Holocaust.
The children are first to be trampled in the frenzy like little, screaming hollyhocks.
Has our flash photography rekindled your instincts? Be the ringmaster

Malefactor   milking every last iamb
From the wound? Did he who made the lamb?

IN THE STACK OF EMPLOYEE SELF-EVALUATIONS

How like you these mine pre-rejection note gathereds
Unblotto auto bi ogre-aphy hazards?
How like you mine glamour shots? Loosely tied robe
Peaking leprose decreprose in patrol car strobe

Twilight (cuff me officer, make
Me make no sudden movements). How *like* you—this discontinued
Merchandise! Slight resemblance in the sinews,
The faulty parts that will one day cease to shake.

I have been squeezing this rock for two
Decades plus, but no water. Just pus
And this gangster rapper thank you curtsey.
I had been squeezing this rock for you
Stranger, God, etc. My work has bound me thus:
Collected, selected, forgotten. And thirsty.

KISSMARRIAGE

Give them, O Lord: what wilt thou give? give
them a miscarrying womb and dry breasts.   —Hosea

Dead baby; shaken, not stirred. Dead baby—
Do not disturb. From happy meal to happy
Hour: dead baby. I'll tell you when you're older.
From a staunch belief in the martial art of spanking,

To the raunchéd grief in the marital altar, *thanking*
Me for this when you're older. I am the tribe elder
And the dead baby inside your dead belly. I am childproof. I say the dar
Ndest things. Expecting mothers

Breed disappointments and I am the father of modern
Dead Babyism. Don't make me pull this carriage over.
Don't make this honeymoon last forever,
This honey mood swing like fists at lovers' first trimesters.

Hush little baby. How far along was she? By the power invested in me, I pronounce you
Dead on arrival. You may mourn the loss.

DYING WORDS

I want a raise. I want a divorce. I want You.
I want to be free. I want you to keep this.
I want to be good in bed. I want to be black. I want to
Win. I want the biggest one you've got. I want justice.

I want to rock and roll all night. I want to kiss you all over.
I want to be where the people are. I want candy.
I want to rock with you. I want to be your lover.
I want to be sedated. I want you to want me.

I want my MTV. I want my daughter back.
I want AIDS. I want my brother's wife. I want to be pretty.
I want a midget. I want my daddy.
I want to puke. I want to go home now. I want a rematch.

I want of a better word. I want to go to college.
I want my money back. I want an apology.

SECTION VIII:

BLUES SONNNET

For Peggy

"for they shall be comforted"
Matthew 5:4

We rent our trousers, but that's the fashion.
We smote our goat, but you're vegetarian.
We masqueraded in fecal cosmetics,
Snarled and growled in canine rhetoric,

We caked on the crematoria and still! Our name
Brand sackcloth is sooo last year. We maim
Our temples, kneel on marbles, we drag
Nails through cheeks, we bum rush body bags,

Caskets...to know a veil.   I pulverized the cross to kindling.
I whittled my face to skull. I took one for the team
Until cartoon stars orbited my diadem in a ring.
I took a Cleveland steamer to the bare bosom but still sing

Those gone but not forgottens. Dearly beloved, our wrists slit
Themselves in protest. And they're being optimistic.

An idea's value depreciates the moment
You drive it off the lot. More proof this "literature"
Fad passes with each iamb. Peppermint
Schnapps complements uninsured Hummers like an over

Eager metrosexual. But it's just a waning
Gibbous briefly waxing poetic. How long till each strophe
Degrades to diluvian Pop culture references? Aging trophy
Husband, virgin waxed Brazilian—why

Do we invest so recklessly in stock pronounced a plummet?
This yacht has sailed. If there's such thing as love
At first sight. If there's such thing as out of sight and out of
Fashion, you're Go-Go boots, love. When your pulse summits,

The EKG tweets "sell" in Morse code
Through gold fronts. And it's going: once. twice.   sold.

MY MOM IS DEAD

for Peggy Martin

In a radical trend of ostentation, avant
Guardians lose their found art. Benefactors invest
Faith arbitrarily. But faith, too, is lost,
As memory. Thus, I remember the last place I put neither. In a recent

Blow to the academy's credibil
Ity, a Mayan child mistakenly discovered volumes of puns
On which translators had given up hope. The vanguard responds un
Favorably, adopting forms oh-so-accessible.

My audience cannot help but retrieve meanings centuries recondite.
Let him go, man. Let him go. Let him go
Claim an undiscovered country in our name, erasing its people
Like a textbook passage. One experimental historian writes,

"I will never get laid.   Ever." The pioneers of this yaw
Found their voices only by blaring them raw.

ROCK STAR AUBADE

for Matt Specht

Nocturnia acquiesces to day. Not *fifteen* and *fame*—quartzite and lumen.
Formica and apple core, halved (aerial view). My shiny chains go jingle jangle.
Through pines, light spangles
The duff cluttered moss; a slot canyon slurps its allotment.   The denim

Asunder, symbolic. Strategic.   Minstrel
Blind as love.   The name of this poem means "crack addict." That barel
Y buttoned blouse is more reveal
Ing than you think. Let's do this—reeval

Uate your priorities.   The sun is a big, blonde morning
Shit God flushes, once more, through his king
Dom. You have bent the exclamation of your fashion s
Tatement into a dead designer question's

Scoliosis.   This poem is named after you, like a slave.   Let the spring
Smolder   Melt your cosmetics   Sing for me Caedmon   Sing!

F.

INSIGHT LIKE RIOT

VIEW FROM A BALCONY

for Sarah Corso

Wow. How do you follow that? Perhaps with a procession
Of mourners, a light reception.
An apology. You heard it here first, folks. The entry-level wages
War, the narcissist plays strip solitaire and wins. Pages

Slip from this binding as if it were a balcony.
I just want to be beautiful. I'm not joking.
I just want to secrete some hatchling
So unrepulsive even my grandmother could be

Indifferent. Is that asking too much and, if so,
Doesn't asking this further question just make matters worse? No.
It makes anti-matters better.   A spinach leaf. The bread
Aisle. Our finest flamingos in the most natural of pinks.   Go ahead

And disgorge. I'll hold back your hair. Like lovers, we two; obscene.
Rest your weary head, which is a chip, on this shoulder. Which is a guillotine.

HALF-FULL BEDPAN

for Valerie Laken

Generosity makes me uncom
Fortable. Their disfigurements make them collectable. I am in love with you or some
One not unlike you.   Everyone and their mom
Must go.   Go demagnetize your moral com

Pass, go prepay after dark, sanguine. If everybody were handicapped,
We'd treat everyone like handicapped
People. If I paid taxes,
I could write this off on my taxes.

The defendant pleads guiltier than you or I could imagine, your honor. There's snow
In my mailbox. But it, too, will melt. Nick
Demske, you have kissed two girls in your life and one
Has since become a faggot. The other died on impact.

Ah Life! You hander of lemons. Never foreseeing their juice
Would quench your pap-iris lacerations thus.

PRISM BREAK

for Frank

There is no zen in history. Just a pronoun and a simile
For parable. Before the workday is over, I will have permanently
Altered this skyline. This just in.
Run don't walk. These beer goggles rearrange my reflection

Into a sexy protagonist. Incessantly positive
Test results. High-rises wildly embr
Acing like dominoes.   There's gotta be a way out of here.   Causative
And effect. Shackles and chains. "No centering Om," Fr.

Time tells the monk.   Nick Demske, you are the most beautiful girl in the World
Trade Center, when refracted through adequate spectrums. I for
Got to eat today. I am incapable of justifying my love for
You. Here is the best offering we have to burn, which disproves the old

Truth   it's the thought that counts. But I shatter the glass only
To mend it reordered.   That I might yet transcend this old mantra   Forgive me.

WRONGO

Or I'll kill you. Or I'll have yo
U killed. Or you'll never see your precious Mongo
Again. If you have received this message in error,
Respond immediately. If you incapacitate the stretcher bearer,

An angel gets its water wings, a rite of passage
Found retarded by scholars. A wrong   of passage. Put me
In coach. Coach; take me back out, coach. Take me very, very
Out. Take anything, mister, just don't hurt the kids   If you received this massage

In error, expect the unhappiest ending. Nick Dems
Ke, you captain of the metaphorical cheerleading squad—your
Greatest achievement in life has been disappointing your
Parents, even to this day, which scholars agree is impressive since

Your mother died weeks ago. You pacifist's arsenal. You war on terror.
It's funny until someone incapacitates the stretcher bearer.

FRANK PSYCHOTIC MANIFESTATION

Methylprednisolone is a glucocorticoid. Glucocorticoids
Are adrenocortical steroids (inactive properties magnesium
Stearate, microcrystalline cellulose and sodium starch
Glycolate), for ankylosing spandylitis and acute, nonspecific tenosynovitis.

I like big words. I'm smart as fuck. I look
In the Kleenex. I look in the toilet.   Among disorders
Hematological: idiopathic thrombocytopenia purpura, congenital
(erythroid) hypoplastic anemia, secondary thrombocytopenia in

Adults and Erythromblastopenia A.   I love you.
I want you. I shave my nipples. I eat a lot.   This shit
Is bananas.   11 Beta, 17, 21-trihydroxy-6alpha-methylpregna-1,
4-diene-3, 20-dione   is our middle name. We all saw this once

In a movie; hold on.   Between the lines, there comes crashing a blow
Near as low
As this brow.

BOWDLER-DASH

for Dave Geisler

Stay out of grown folks' business. Do not stare at the burn on her
Face. Do not stare at the views and opinions expressed here
Are not necessarily the views and opinions of Nick Demske, the quaint, cowed,
Cupcake of a schoolboy. The French toast begging your pardon. Say it loud:

"I'm white and I'm ashamed!" I'm a tramp on the streets and a Jesus freak
In the bed. Don't ask stupid questions? At a low, low price?   Point and click.
Shuck and Jive.   Do you want to feel
My scars? My sweet topography, like rubberized Braille?
I thought you'd never ask.

                              I wouldn't. Nor tell.
Do not look directly at the poem. Offer val
Id only at participating locations. MF
A. Slave dialect. I want your native tongue in the recess

Es of my throat like I want to command a better mastery of the patriarch's all potent
Argot.   Alls I'm trying to say is   [*section omitted*]

NEGRO SPIRITUAL

for Dayvin

The only thing fair about God is his skin.
Sorry to rain on your million man march.
If you're in my country, you ought speak the King
Of kings English. You ought lynch your collar starched.

This neighborhood used to be so nice. Now the rat race riots asphyxiate its aqueducts.
Racism is colorblind, like my once living mother singing from her hymnal; the whitest
White person to ever feel entitled. What's
The universal sign for choking on the Eucharist?

This blank page I made you is a colored pencil
Mural of a wafer so hoar it'll choke the demons out us all. [revise: "pencil
Of color" –Ed.] In the beginning, there was the N-word,
With colorblind faith in forty acres, a mule. God wins because he's bigger,

Until I digest this cracker, converting it on
Into the drabbest defecant His face will ever don.

GOOD TOUCH

after Walt Disney

This is the most beautiful stool sample I have ever see
N. A stool sampler could search her whole life for a specimen half this perfect.
I can't taste this food. I can't feel my legs.
You must feel them for me. You suppository.

The emancipated marionette snips its own strings. This confirms its inab
Ility to move independent. Can you show me on the puppet where
The poetry touched you? Would you like to sample some of our
Finest stool, today? I need an adult. I need an ad

Olescent—a sweater puppeteer shiver me tim
Bers. "That poetry touched me," my virgin ears bleed.
"I was moved by your puppetry," my bowels fess, ashamed.
The incontinent coprophile wallows in bliss. A pedophile wets the bed. Kiss me like I'm

Still a child, a Real Boy, proclaiming this, the finest stool sample of its kind,
The finest the world has seen since the great sampling of ought nine.

CRÈME IN CREMATORIUM

The damsel screaming upon the tracks.
It's my day off. Off what? Medication. Birth control.
The slumber party turned traumatic when they slipped their sleeping
Friend's hand into water and, instead of wetting herself, she burst into

Flames. I love you so much that I jumped
Off a roof I could not see the ground from. I salt all my food
Before tasting it. Miniature thongs in the juniors department.
Pop rocks and soda. Seagulls and Alka-Seltzer.

My student ID still yields the discount despite its
Having expired. If you love homosexuals so much,
Why don't you marry them? A salary commensurate with the candidates
Qualifications. Don't take off the heels. Don't take

Off the gauze. My penis is the answer to your vagina.
Your vagina was rhetorical.

GOOD OL' WAGON

There is a tree that leans toward lightning.
There is a sand that sweats into glass.
There is a dove in love with cage fighting.
There is a poem, crumpled and trashed.

I compose eulogies for the living. Jokes
For species that don't speak laughter.
I write flower print checks and imbalances
That bounce flyer than hearse hydraulics.

"It supports abortion because it wishes its mother
Had had one." Instead an ink baptism anoints
The stillborn fetus. Brotherly lover,
Cursèd weilder of incontinent ball points,

I'd say you don' broke down but this
Would imply you'd left the factory fixed.

THEM BACKSTABBERS

for Anne Shaw

When you knighted me, the falchion crashed down upon my
Chine. Banishèd, the chrysalis. Banishèd, the simian, choleric aberrat
Ions. Revolutionized, the art
Of child pornography.   *My baby. Won't somebody*

Please save my baby.   For translating the works of broken
Blenders into English, the Academy fits this upstart with a person
Alized letterman's straightjacket.   Boy,   it's really
Coming down now. But of course that's when power lines palsy most thespian. I really

Shouldn't. You really shouldn't have.   I haven't   understood a single
Poem I've written in one hundred fiscal
Years. But damn, these hedges. Impeccable. Will breaks like a word caught between
Two lines of verse.   "How to autotomize the ivory in these tusks?" "When

Did my pen so turn upon itself?" I yelp and spasm, crying,
(Wah) until a revelation.   I unsheathe the wet quill from my spine.

FEELS NO PAIN

for Dave Demske

> *"nor eats, nor hungers"*
> —Melville

The kind of love you only read about in fairy tales.
The kind of self-hatred you only acknowledge in poetry.
The Lord taketh and the Lord giveth away.

SECTION THE 7TH.

BLACK STAR

With unrestrained alacrity, the mainstream
Bleaches its anus. Savory loblolly hologram
Summers.   I like banjos.   I like
It'll grow back.   You are the first black

Person I have ever met in real life.   This
Alcove a strobe so ablaze with resplendence
The sun itself cast doth a shadow!   O my nasty God.
Votive pyromania.   You people.

As white as the presidential race itself.   You have snapped thrice in a Z
Formation.   You have a sex so rough it's concept
Ual rape.   *   If I'm never afforded a Borealis, at least let me
Witness a meth lab explode before I die, shiny trinkets

Marring my pedicured lawn, my neatly spaced shing
Les, my cloture so blanched it brings sight to the blind.

EAT SHIT AND DIE

"especially the being through"

—*Berryman*

You are the warden of my heart. My homeland security blanket
Policy. And those buttes frame the valley like epaulettes on an unclouded
Decapitatee.   The poor man's doorbell. The poor man's welcome mat.
You are my favorite poet. Let's go poke dead

Stuff with sticks.   Coppices hud
Dling like a flatland's downtown. In lieu of the oven and like technologies,
Ostriches bury their heads in beach.   I have surrendered my keys
Unto a bowl for my spouse and the much greater good

Of this party. The poor man's
Camping. The only pitch we label perfect. Your janitorial
Services are no longer needed here, like nature when we've remote starting vehicles.
The dead stuff inevitably starts to poke back. The moon's drunken

Simper tries to sell us a car. And succeeds. My demands for the life of your
Precious, precious Mongo mimic my long term goals. They follow in no particular order:

PROFUNDITY

"two letters traced by a hoof in the dust,"
                                        —Ovid

A sequence of Ms denotes palatability, the ability to pal
At, if you will. But you won't. Out of a principle
Void of all *pal.* The charges have been
Dropped to the depths for which they were named. The *art* in in

Articulate. The *ysis* in analysis. Sadly, I have to remain a god.   A sequence
Of Zs denotes slumber, lest precede
D by a lone B, then indicating a creature whose only defense
Is suicide. Do you have any idea what we're de

Aling with, here? The *angel* in televangelist. The neolo
Gism. You can't escape form. Belie
Ve me. I've tried. An alternating sequence of Xs and Os
Designates male cows, the toes of tic tackery

But, beyond that—our love, near as golden
As the showers which bear that name. *MMMM.*

THE TRAFFIC SLOWS IN PASSING

for Anne Callaghan

> *"Death is the mother"*
> —*Wallace Stevens*

The orgy participants jockey for position.
The arboretum explodes with the splendor of a Molotov.
You are beautiful. So naked beneath the chicken
Suit; the exact and menacing dance moves.

I want to dehumanize you in a poem. Objectify you like a woman.
The orgy participants explode with the splendor of autumn,
A synonym for education. They press their hands toward each other on either
Side of the glass, so shatter resistant. The drunk driver

Makes an abstraction of our loved one, a sculpture of our mid-sized fam
Ily sedan.
If we are ever left alone in an empty room
There will occur an interaction so palpably indecent, the flowers will bloom

Out of season. *Have you ever felt this alone,* I whisper, lost
Running all eight of my fingers through all eight of your hairs.   Almost.

PREGNANT CHAD

Vote yes on this ballot and get a free
Abortion when you purchase any additional abortion of equal or lesser
Of two evils. Honk if you're saving yourself for marriage. Hear ye
Sinners; he clave the rock and the waters

Menstruated forth like a head wound—no, a
Boil on Job's ass! Vote yes if you're not chicken.
Bu bawk bawk bawwwk.   This poem paid for by the
People that brought you natural selection,

Epidurals and baby bibs
With Noah's ark graphics stitched on. Vote yes and choose to give
A child Life. Vote yes for
Promotional use only, vote yes sir, right away sir,

Vote yes if you love me, vote yes, vote yes, vote yes
Yes, yes, no please don't stop   I was so close.

O, REVOLUTION

All counter revolutionaries are asked to leave
The party. All revolutionaries must wash hands. All circuits
Are currently busy and all I got was this lousy need
Le. In my all. The revolution deposits

Us back at the start, like all revolutions all tuckered out all opposed? Abstentions? And
The motion passes away in its sleep. But at this rate
Of interest, the revolution runs unaffordable for any povert
Of your tax bracket. United we stand

For nothing. Divided we f
All.   4   1   Achtung, Achtung. All revolutionar
Ies to the throne must report to their supervisors at once, like a dog returneth
To his master's tools. I learned to love going in circles on care

O-cells, learned to love chasing my tail in Fall. The revolution, in all, will be
         (parenthetical).
And if you dismantle the masterpiece?   Will that be all?

PSA

The terrorist was last seen noogieing leukemia
Patients. The terrorist was last seen zerberting fat
Babies. I hate to be the bearer of accurate news, but that
Wiley ol' terrorist was recently spotted perfecting taxidermia

On the decapitated Head of State.   All calls
Are being monitored for quality assurance purposes.
A stars and barcode has been installed
For our convenience. The representative from Indiana proposes

This moratorium on warning shots last indefinitely.
The terrorist was last seen evading its taxes.
The terrorist was last seen profiling A-rabs. With greatly
Exaggerated ease, the terrorist teeters upon its axis

Of piety, doubledutching the loopholes of the laws.
The terrorist hates our freedom. The terrorist loves the applause.

ECDYSIAST POETRY

for Sara Thornton

> *"the answer to all those rhetorical questions"*
> —*Nick Demske*

A finger contours the serrations. A hand with all its digits
Intact caresses these stumps with a wash rag. This is
All my fault. I never should have let this happen.
So liberated we voluntarily bind our librations

Inside this cage; its dimension lines a high art form, throbbing out our rhythm.
She sways like the bangs of a willow. With her bamboo manicure.
With your skin shell hide husk rind etc.   But I'll never die because I am
A god. You, on the other hand, are

Female. It's so cold the snow looks like diamonds. If we're
So frickin' beautiful,   we'll shove our lily hands into the contents
Of this diaper here and mould them to a song. We'll burrow deeper
Into all our thickly caked integuments, just to dim our radiance's violent,

Seismic vox.   Undistorted majesty demands
It's own grotesqueness.   It's so cold the coal looks like diamonds.

MISGUIDED POLITICS

The end justifies the widow.
You always have to be right.
 She dangles there like a leftover no
One will ever digest. I write

What's left of her: these conservative wings, these margins,
 violently indented. If this hand be sinister, I shall cup it o'er my heart
   like the Romans, With justice for all. But the ambidexterity
Reveals my indecision and Chinese people read

Stuff backwards.   The means justifies the widow, self-righteous
Fourteener allegiance. Loosey; tighty—all mis
Direction leads to the same perfect
Circle.   This is war.   So this song, like the others, will ever be left

Unjustified, haw, right to its very last line.   Gee.
This is the first line of the poem.   eeee.

THEY ALL LIVED

The purpose has officially been
Defeated. Our disbelief has been suspend
Ded   indefinitely. I have hyper-extended my met
Aphor like gold to airy thinness beat.

I have mixed these metaphors
Into a batter that burns like some multicult
Ural miscegeny *thing*. What a bull summoned I to this sheet like a matador.
Expecting to cello its throat.

The purpose waves a blank page. Our disbelief's feet jangle from a gal
Lows, eyes bulging.   I just want my life back.
Die, motherfucker, die.   Nick Demske, you've been rattling the bars
Of an unlocked cage. You're the president of the anarchy club.   Tell

My wife and kids that I love them very much. The view fr
Om these horns is breathtaking.   Happily ever after.

I.

HEZEKIAH ENVOI

FULLY DRESSED IN AN EMPTY BATHTUB

for Francisco and for Peggy

From this clock tower, the people look like little ants,
Whispers my giant magnifier. Below the noose, at
The trunk of the tree, they found two packs of cigarette
Butts. But they never found a body. Tonite, I want to do something permanent,

Something undoable. I want to kiss you
And reveal my secret feelings for you. For a long time I considered
Hating everything in the world. Instead, I decided
To huff it. All of it. Porcelain. Impotence. The taste of wounds.

The moment before the mistake.   We draw ponies.
Over and over again, to keep the fires of hell
At bay. Pretty ponies. The kind that paralyze you beneath
The generous weight of their bodies. I could've killed

Myself that night, but instead I plucked these shards from my flesh, licked
The lacerations. Fashioned this glowing mosaic.

NICK DEMSKE works at
the Racine Public Library.
His writing appears in
*Action Yes, Sawbuck, The
Bathroom Magazine, Fact-
Simile, Blazevox, Moria*
and *Queef*. He curates the
BONK! performance series
in Racine and is editor of
the online forum *boo: a
journal of terrific things*.

Fence Books supports writers who might otherwise have difficulty being recognized because their work doesn't answer to either the mainstream or to recognizable modes of experimentation.

The Motherwell Prize is an annual series that offers publication of a first or second book of poems by a woman, as well as a five thousand dollar cash prize.

The Fence Modern Poets Series contest is open to poets of any gender and at any stage of career, and offers a one thousand dollar cash prize in addition to book publication.

For more information about either prize, or about *Fence*, visit www. fenceportal.org.

Fence books